P9-BJJ-901

EVERY DAY A
HOLY DAY

Daily Prayer Journal

Published by The Word Among Us Press
7115 Guilford Drive
Frederick, Maryland 21704
www.wau.org

23 22 21 20 19   1 2 3 4 5

ISBN: 978-1-59325-231-1

Design by Suzanne Earl

Printed in China

All of us, gazing with unveiled face on the glory of the Lord,
are being transformed into the same image from glory to glory,
as from the Lord who is the Spirit.

—2 CORINTHIANS 3:18

Dear Friend in Christ,

If you ask people why they keep prayer journals, you'll get a variety of answers. "It helps me clarify my thoughts and be more honest with God." "When I see how God has answered my prayers, it builds my trust." "It keeps me focused on what matters." Essentially, all the reasons boil down to this: a prayer journal is a tool for deepening your relationship with the Lord. The title of this prayer journal gets right to the heart of it: *Every Day a Holy Day.*

As the Scripture passage above makes clear, each day is an opportunity to be transformed into the image of the Lord . . . to be holy! In this journal, you'll find a quotation from a saint or other spiritual writer and ample space for writing, along with beautiful images to inspire your prayer and journaling time.

This prayer journal is your spiritual diary, a private communication between you and the Lord. It's the place where you can pour out your thoughts to him.

What do you write? Anything that touches or moves you spiritually: God's word and your response, ordinary happenings at work or at home, your joys and triumphs, pain and frustration, events both small and great. A journal helps you keep track of what happens as you sit with the Lord and ponder what he is saying to you through Scripture and your experiences.

Begin your prayer journal by making a few choices. First, decide when you will pray (preferably, the same time each day) and where (a place that is quiet and free of distractions).

When you pray, quiet your thoughts. If it's helpful, light a candle or listen to some music. Out loud or in the stillness of your heart, invite Jesus to be with you. There's no formula for what to do or when. You might read Scripture—next Sunday's Gospel, perhaps, or a psalm. Or just talk to the Lord about whatever is on your mind. Then, be sure to listen. Sometimes, it will seem that nothing happens. Other times, you may sense the strong presence of the Lord. Recording such times in a prayer journal not only helps you to remember them but also lets you see the depth of the love the Lord has for you. This builds your faith and helps you get through the times when your prayer is dry and you don't feel the Lord speaking to you.

As you read Scripture during prayer, one or two lines may jump out at you. It's as if the Lord is speaking to you directly, and the passage may have something important to say to you. At these times, it's helpful simply to write down the Scripture passage that spoke to you. It may be something you need to carry with you throughout the day, and writing it down will help you to remember it or find it again easily. By going back and rereading the passage later on in your journal, you can remember why God wanted to speak that word to you.

There are so many ways you can use a prayer journal. You can write down prayer petitions and then write down how God has answered them. You can mark important days, like birthdays, anniversaries, or other special events in the life of your family. You can record prayers of the Church that you love, writings of the saints that have inspired you, or some insight about a relationship you may have had. Journaling need not be another chore, something you "should" do. When you have prayed, if you have a pen and journal in hand, you can be ready to write down whatever has inspired you. If you have nothing to write, you can simply put down two words: "I prayed."

The Word Among Us Press

PRAYER NOTES

JANUARY

The only way to make rapid progress along the path of divine love is to remain very little and to put all our trust in Almighty God. That is what I have done.

—ST. THÉRÈSE OF LISIEUX

To you we entrust . . . the future of the Church, the future of humanity. Mary, Mother of God, Queen of Peace, watch over us.

—ST. JOHN PAUL II

1

_____

_____

_____

_____

_____

_____

_____

_____

_____

Intimacy with the Lord is not a matter of physical kinship; rather, it is achieved by cheerful readiness to do the will of God.

—ST. BASIL

2

_____

_____

_____

_____

_____

_____

_____

_____

Oh, how great is your Name, O Lord! It is the strength of my soul. When my strength fails, and darkness invades my soul, your Name is the sun whose rays give lights and also warmth.

—ST. FAUSTINA KOWALSKA

3

The first end I propose in our daily work is to do the Will of God; secondly, to do it in the manner he wills it; and thirdly, to do it because it is his Will.

—ST. ELIZABETH ANN SETON

4

JANUARY

Though God hates sin more than any other thing, he loves us poor miserable sinners. He ardently desires the welfare of our souls as if his own happiness depended on it.

—ST. JOHN NEUMANN

5

Our Lord is our big Brother, and we are the little brothers. Consequently, we should love one another as members of the same family.

—ST. ANDRÉ BESSETTE

6

May God shelter you from disturbance in the hidden recesses of his love, until he brings you at last into that place of fullness where you will repose forever in the vision of peace.

—ST. RAYMOND OF PEÑAFORT

7

Cast yourself into the arms of God and be very sure that if he wants anything of you, he will fit you for the work and give you strength.

—ST. PHILIP NERI

8

JANUARY

We shall steer safely through every storm,
so long as our heart is right, our intention fervent,
our courage steadfast, and our trust fixed in God.

—ST. FRANCIS DE SALES

9

It is only when everything is hopeless that hope
begins to be a strength at all. Like all the Christian
virtues, it is as unreasonable as it is indispensable.

—G. K. CHESTERTON

10

He said not: You shall not be troubled—
you shall not be tempted—you shall not be
distressed. But he said: You shall not be overcome.

—BLESSED JULIAN OF NORWICH

_____

_____

_____

11

_____

_____

_____

_____

_____

With the confidence of a son, rest in the care and
love that Divine Providence has for you in all your
needs. Look upon Providence as a child does its
mother who loves him tenderly. You can be sure that
God loves you incomparably more.

—ST. JANE FRANCES DE CHANTAL

_____

_____

12

_____

_____

_____

_____

_____

JANUARY

God, fill with wind the sails I have hoisted for you, and carry me forward on my course.

—ST. HILARY

13

I will remember how St. Peter, at a blast of wind, began to sink because of his lack of faith, and I will do as he did: call upon Christ and pray to him for help. And then I trust he will place his holy hand on me and in the stormy seas hold me up from drowning.

—ST. THOMAS MORE

14

Hope always draws the soul from the beauty that is seen to what is beyond, always kindles the desire for the hidden through what is perceived.

—ST. GREGORY OF NYSSA

15

The heart of God invites all to put it to the proof. The more he gives, the more he desires to give. He loves to see the trust which makes us persist in knocking unceasingly.

—BLESSED PLACID RICCARDI

16

JANUARY

> He who knows himself knows all men.
> He who can love himself loves all men.
>
> —ST. ANTHONY OF EGYPT

17

> The only way to make rapid progress along
> the path of divine love is to remain very little
> and to put all our trust in Almighty God.
> That is what I have done.
>
> —ST. THÉRÈSE OF LISIEUX

18

The greater and more persistent your confidence
in God, the more abundantly you will receive
all that you ask.

—ST. ALBERT THE GREAT

19

Cast your cares upon God, for you are his
and he will not forget you.

—ST. JOHN OF THE CROSS

20

JANUARY

Christ has made my soul beautiful
with the jewels of grace and virtue.
I belong to him whom the angels serve.

—ST. AGNES

21

The deepest element of God's commandment to
protect human life is the requirement to show
reverence and love for every person and the life
of every person.

—POPE ST. JOHN PAUL II

22

f your confidence were as great as it ought to be, you
would not worry about what may happen to you; you
ould place it all in God's hands, hoping that when he
ants something of you, he will let you know what it is.

—ST. CLAUDE DE LA COLOMBIÈRE

2 3

There is nothing small in the service of God.

—ST. FRANCIS DE SALES

2 4

JANUARY

The same Jesus who touched Saul is ready
and able to transform each of us,
setting us on fire with his love.

—A YEAR OF CELEBRATION

25

_____
_____
_____
_____
_____
_____
_____

[God] saved us, not because of deeds done by us
in righteousness, but in virtue of his own mercy,
by the washing of regeneration and renewal
in the Holy Spirit.

—TITUS 3:5 (RSVCE)

26

_____
_____
_____
_____
_____
_____
_____

In order to become an instrument in God's hands,
we must be of no account in our own eyes.

—ST. ANGELA MERICI

27

_____

Grant me, O Lord my God, a mind to know you,
a heart to seek you, wisdom to find you,
conduct pleasing to you, faithful perseverance
in waiting for you, and a hope
of finally embracing you.

—ST. THOMAS AQUINAS

28

JANUARY

God is full of compassion, and never fails those who
are afflicted and despised, if they trust in him alone.

—ST. TERESA OF ÁVILA

29

Have great confidence in Jesus, and may your
trust in him grow daily. . . . Lean on your Beloved,
because the soul who abandons herself in the hands
of Jesus in all she does is carried in his arms.

—ST. FRANCES CABRINI

30

Believe me . . . nobody can be truly happy in this world unless he is at peace with God.

—ST. JOHN BOSCO

31

PRAYER NOTES

JANUARY

FEBRUARY

Our hearts should each day seek a resting place on Calvary or near our Lord, in order to retire there to rest from worldly cares and to find strength against temptation.

—ST. FRANCIS DE SALES

Without work, it's impossible to have fun.

—ST. THOMAS AQUINAS

1

The Mother of God, the most pure Virgin, carried the true light in her arms and brought him to those who lay in darkness. We too should carry a light for all to see and reflect the radiance of the true light as we hasten to meet him.

—ST. SOPHRONIUS

2

Grace is nothing else but a certain beginning
of glory in us.

—ST. THOMAS AQUINAS

3

Mercy is the fulfillment of justice, not its abolition.

—ST. THOMAS AQUINAS

4

FEBRUARY

Jesus Christ, Lord of all . . . I am your sheep:
make me worthy to overcome the devil.

—ST. AGATHA

5

After Christ's example, I forgive my persecutors.

—ST. PAUL MIKI

6

In your work or sorrow, never forget we have a great reward stored up for us in Heaven.

—ST. JOHN BOSCO

7

I have given everything to my Master: He will take care of me. . . . The best thing for us is not what we consider best, but what the Lord wants of us!

—ST. JOSEPHINE BAKHITA

8

FEBRUARY

What tenderness there is in Jesus' love for man!
In his infinite goodness, he established, with each
of us, bonds of sublime love! His love has no limits

—ST. JOHN BOSCO

9

I asked you and you would not listen;
so I asked my God and he did listen.

—ST. SCHOLASTICA

10

Grant, most tender of mothers, that I may be a child
after your own heart and that of your divine Son.

—ST. BERNADETTE SOUBIROUS

11

Christ alone is my life and my salvation.

—ST. AGATHA

12

FEBRUARY

I can truly say that it was a miracle I did not die,
because the Lord has destined me for greater things.

—ST. JOSEPHINE BAKHITA

13

O Lord my God, . . . build up your church
and gather all into unity.

—ST. CYRIL

14

It is because I am weak that I dare to receive God, who is strong.

—ST. BERNADETTE SOUBIROUS

15

O Lord my God, . . . inspire the hearts of your people with your word and your teaching.

—ST. CYRIL

16

FEBRUARY

They loved God above all things and dedicated
their whole lives to him by honoring him
in their every thought, word and deed.

—AN ACCOUNT OF THE ORIGIN
OF THE SERVITE ORDER

17

Following the example of Jesus,
I will carry the cross with
courage and generosity.

—ST. BERNADETTE SOUBIROUS

18

Let Christ always abide in your heart
by the fire of his love.

—ST. PETER DAMIAN

19

He who has charity is far from all sin.

—ST. POLYCARP

20

FEBRUARY

Each one of the faithful is, so to speak,
the Church in miniature.

—ST. PETER DAMIAN

21

Let us thank God together for founding his Church
on the rock of Peter. . . . Let us pray intensely that
amid the upheavals of the world, she may not be
shaken but advance with courage and trust.

—POPE ST. JOHN PAUL II

22

Help one another with the generosity of the Lord, and despise no one. When you have the opportunity to do good, do not let it go by.

—ST. POLYCARP

23

Give way to one another in the Lord's own spirit of courtesy, treating no one as inferior.

—ST. POLYCARP

24

FEBRUARY

Our hearts should each day seek a resting place on Calvary or near our Lord, in order to retire there to rest from worldly cares and to find strength against temptation.

—ST. FRANCIS DE SALES

25

Have you run so many circles of the years bustling vainly about the world, and have you not forty days to be free for prayer for your own soul's sake?

—ST. CYRIL OF JERUSALEM

26

May your faith be increased so as to realize
the fact that you are never alone, wheresoever you
may be, that the great God is with you, in you.

—ST. KATHARINE DREXEL

_____
_____
_____   **27**
_____
_____
_____
_____
_____
_____

We are called to be saints, all of us;
do not forget that.

—ST. KATHARINE DREXEL

_____
_____
_____   **28**
_____
_____
_____
_____
_____

FEBRUARY

> Let your heart delight in the love your God has for you, personally, individually.
>
> —ST. KATHARINE DREXEL

29

PRAYER NOTES

PRAYER NOTES

FEBRUARY

MARCH

Lord, keep your grace in my heart. Live in me so that your grace be mine. Make it that I may bear every day some flowers and new fruit.

—ST. GIANNA BERETTA MOLLA

Love the poor tenderly, regarding them as your
masters and yourselves as their servants.

—ST. JOHN OF GOD

1

We owe three things to God: love, service, reverence

—ST. JOHN OF GOD

2

You have no time to occupy your thoughts with that complacency or consideration of what others will think. Your business is simply, "What will my Father in heaven think?"

—ST. KATHARINE DREXEL

3

Charity commits us principally to love God's will above all things.

—ST. LOUISE DE MARILLAC

4

MARCH

How good it is to trust God! Turn to Him often,
as children look to their father and mother
in their needs.

—ST. LOUISE DE MARILLAC

5

If you keep good companions, I can assure you that
you will one day rejoice with the blessed in Heaven,
whereas if you keep with those who are bad, you will
become bad yourself, and you will be in danger of
losing your soul.

—ST. JOHN BOSCO

6

Stand fast in the faith, and love one another.
—ST. PERPETUA

7

_____
_____
_____
_____
_____
_____
_____
_____

We owe three things to God: love, service, reverence.
—ST. JOHN OF GOD

8

_____
_____
_____
_____
_____
_____
_____

MARCH

Turn trustingly to the Lord who is my God and
put your faith in him with all your heart,
because nothing is impossible to him.

—ST. PATRICK

9

Whatever will come my way, whether good or bad,
I may accept it calmly, and always give thanks to
God, who has ever shown me how I should believe
in him unfailing without end.

—ST. PATRICK

10

All for God and for his glory. In whatever you do, think of the glory of God as your main goal.

—ST. JOHN BOSCO

11

_____

_____

_____

_____

_____

_____

_____

_____

_____

The proper effect of the Eucharist is the transformation of man into God.

—ST. THOMAS AQUINAS

12

_____

_____

_____

_____

_____

_____

_____

MARCH

Great deeds may not always come our way,
but at all times we can do little deeds
with perfection, that is, with love.

—ST. FRANCIS DE SALES

13

_____

_____

_____

_____

_____

_____

_____

_____

Hope everything from the mercy of God.
It is as boundless as his power.

—ST. FRANCES OF ROME

14

_____

_____

_____

_____

_____

_____

_____

The trouble you've gone to won't be wasted:
after the rain, the sun shines out!

—ST. LOUISE DE MARILLAC

15

The chief service I owe you, O God, is that every
thought and word of mine should speak of you.

—ST. HILARY

16

MARCH

I arise today through the strength of Christ
with his baptism, through the strength of his
crucifixion with his burial, through the strength
of his Resurrection with his Ascension.

—ST. PATRICK

17

Your wounds are not greater
than the Physician's skill.

—ST. CYRIL OF JERUSALEM

18

Anyone who cannot find a master to teach him prayer should take this glorious saint [Joseph] for his master, and he will not go astray.

—ST. TERESA OF ÁVILA

19

Love St. Joseph . . . with all your soul, because he, together with Jesus, is the person who has most loved our Blessed Lady and has been closest to God.

—ST. JOSEMARÍA ESCRIVÁ

20

MARCH

Christian husband! . . . Cherish those belonging
to you as the holy foster father did Jesus,
and be their faithful protector.

—ST. JOHN VIANNEY

21

I have never known anyone to be truly devoted
to St. Joseph who did not noticeably advance
in virtue, for he gives very real help to souls
who commend themselves to him.

—ST. TERESA OF ÁVILA

22

Christ with me, Christ before me,
Christ behind me, Christ in me,
Christ beneath me, Christ above me,
Christ on my right, Christ on my left.

—ST. PATRICK'S BREASTPLATE

23

A gentle maiden having lodged a God in her womb,
asks as its price, peace for the world, salvation for
those who are lost, and life for the dead.

—ST. PETER CHRYSOLOGUS

24

MARCH

Our Lady was full of God because she lived for God alone, yet she thought of herself only as the handmaid of the Lord. Let us do the same.

—ST. TERESA OF CALCUTTA

25

After partaking of the Living Bread, remember wha our Lady . . . must have felt when the Holy Spirit overpowered her, and she, Mary, who was full of grace, became full with the body of Christ.

— ST. TERESA OF CALCUTTA

26

Why object to the Son of God made man washing
external dirt from feet, when he who is God
has already humbled himself in order
to wash foulness from souls?

—BLESSED FULTON SHEEN

27

Savior, your crucifixion marked the end
of your mortal life; teach us to crucify ourselves
and make way for our life in the Spirit.

—ST. EPHREM

28

MARCH

The arms of the Crucified are spread out
to draw you to his heart.

—ST. TERESA BENEDICTA
OF THE CROSS (EDITH STEIN)

29
_____
_____
_____

_____
_____
_____
_____
_____

God wishes to be seen, and he wishes to be sought,
and he wishes to be expected, and he wishes
to be trusted.

—BLESSED JULIAN OF NORWICH

30
_____
_____

_____
_____
_____
_____

Lord, keep your grace in my heart. Live in me so that your grace be mine. Make it that I may bear every day some flowers and new fruit.

—ST. GIANNA BERETTA MOLLA

31

PRAYER NOTES

MARCH

APRIL

O Death, where is your sting? O Hell, where is your victory? Christ is risen, and you are overthrown!

—ST. JOHN CHRYSOSTOM

Jesus . . . is for me honor, delight, heart, and soul.
He whom I love is fatherland, heaven already!
My treasure! My love! Jesus, and Jesus
crucified alone makes my happiness.

—ST. BERNADETTE SOUBIROUS

1

In the trials and temptations we face regularly
in our daily lives, help one another.

—ST. FRANCIS OF PAOLA

2

Love above all else our merciful Father in heaven,
and serve him with all your strength
and purity of heart.

—ST. FRANCIS OF PAOLA

3

Reading the holy Scriptures . . . turns man's
attention from the follies of the world
and leads him to the love of God.

—ST. ISIDORE OF SEVILLE

4

APRIL

If you truly want to help the soul of your neighbor, you should approach God first with all your heart. Ask him simply to fill you with charity, the greatest of all virtues; with it you can accomplish what you desire.

—ST. VINCENT FERRER

5

When the soul has seen God, what more can it want? If it possesses him, why and for whom can it ever be moved to abandon him?

—ST. VINCENT FERRER

6

Would we want our own hidden sins to be divulged?
Then we should be silent about
the hidden sins of others.

—ST. JOHN BAPTIST DE LA SALLE

7

It is good when a soul loves solitude;
it's a sign that it takes delight in God
and enjoys speaking with him.

—ST. JANE FRANCES DE CHANTAL

8

APRIL

Jesus, the Crucified, is to be the only object
of your longings, your wishes, your thoughts.

—ST. TERESA BENEDICTA OF THE CROSS
(EDITH STEIN)

9

Look at His adorable face. Look at His glazed
and sunken eyes. Look at His wounds.
Look Jesus in the Face. There, you
will see how He loves us.

—ST. THÉRÈSE OF LISIEUX

10

I confess that I am bewildered and lose myself at the thought of divine goodness, a sea without shore and fathomless, of God who calls me to an eternal rest after such short and tiny labors.

—ST. ALOYSIUS GONZAGA

11

What man, stationed in a foreign land, would not want to return to his own country as soon as possible? . . . O the supreme and endless bliss of everlasting life!

—ST. CYPRIAN

12

APRIL

Our home is—heaven. On earth we are like travelers
staying in a hotel. When one is away,
one is always thinking of going home.

—ST. JOHN VIANNEY

13

There is a human splendor and a celestial splendor.
The splendor that can be attained on earth is
temporary and limited, while that of heaven lasts
forever, which will be shown when the corruptible
becomes incorruptible and the mortal immortal.

—ST. BASIL THE GREAT

14

Blessed are you, my Lord, my God,
for you are unchangeable in all eternity!
Whoever faithfully serves you until the end
shall enjoy life without end in all eternity.

—ST. TERESA OF ÁVILA

_____

_____

_____   **15**

_____

_____

_____

_____

_____

_____

Our rest will be in heaven.
O heaven, heaven, whoever thinks
on you will not suffer from weariness!

—ST. JOSEPH CAFASSO

_____

_____

_____   **16**

_____

_____

_____

_____

_____   **APRIL**

The pleasant companionship of all the blessed in heaven will be a companionship replete with delight.

—ST. THOMAS AQUINAS

17

_____
_____
_____
_____
_____
_____
_____
_____

In heaven, the soul is certain that it loves God, and that He embraces it as a beloved child and that this love shall not be dissolved for all eternity.

—ST. ALPHONSUS LIGUORI

18

_____
_____
_____
_____
_____
_____
_____

And what can one say of all the other blessings of heaven? There will be health, and no sickness; liberty, and no servitude; beauty, and no unsightliness; immortality, and no decay.

—ST. PETER OF ALCÁNTARA

19

_____

_____

_____

_____

_____

_____

_____

_____

Life is passing. Eternity draws nigh: soon shall we live the very life of God. After having drunk deep at the fount of bitterness, our thirst will be quenched at the very source of all sweetness.

—ST. THÉRÈSE OF LISIEUX

20

_____

_____

_____

_____

_____

_____

APRIL

While I am here on earth let me learn
to know you better, so that in heaven I may know
you fully; let my love for you grow deeper here,
so that there I may love you fully.

—ST. ANSELM

21

But, my soul, . . . you cannot deny that after this
life, which flits away like a shadow, if you remain
firm in faith, hope, and love, you will see God
clearly and truly as he is.

—ST. ROBERT BELLARMINE

22

God will not deny his mercy to anyone.
Heaven and earth may change, but God's mercy
will never be exhausted.

—ST. FAUSTINA KOWALSKA

23

_____
_____
_____
_____
_____
_____
_____
_____
_____
_____

O Death, where is your sting?
O Hell, where is your victory? Christ is risen,
and you are overthrown!

—ST. JOHN CHRYSOSTOM

24

_____
_____
_____
_____
_____
_____
_____
_____
_____

APRIL

Just as the soul now finds it impossible to desire unhappiness, so in heaven it shall be wholly impossible for it to desire sin.

—ST. AUGUSTINE OF HIPPO

2 5

The Risen One goes before us and he accompanies us along the paths of the world. He is our hope. He is the true peace of the world.

—POPE BENEDICT XVI

2 6

May the joy of Our Risen Lord be your strength
in your work, your way to the Father,
your light to guide you and your Bread of Life.

—ST. TERESA OF CALCUTTA

27

God is a spring of living water that flows
unceasingly into the hearts of those who pray.

—ST. LOUIS DE MONTFORT

28

APRIL

If you are what you should be, you will set
the whole world on fire.

—ST. CATHERINE OF SIENA

29

Build yourself a cell in your heart
and retire there to pray.

—ST. CATHERINE OF SIENA

30

PRAYER NOTES

APRIL

MAY

Be trustful, firmly believing that God always provides for souls who trust in him.

—ST. CATHERINE OF SIENA

> Joseph turned his human vocation to domestic love into a superhuman oblation of self, an oblation of his heart and all his abilities into love placed at the service of the Messiah growing up in his house.
>
> —ST. PAUL VI

1

_____

> The Son of God became man so that we might become God.
>
> —ST. ATHANASIUS

2

Like every good evangelist, Philip not only spoke
to others about Christ but invited them
to meet him personally.

—POPE BENEDICT XVI

3

_____
_____
_____
_____
_____
_____
_____
_____

His mercy is so great that He has forbidden
none to strive to come and drink of
this fountain of life. Blessed be He forever!

—ST. TERESA OF ÁVILA

4

_____
_____
_____
_____
_____
_____

MAY

Be trustful, firmly believing that God always
provides for souls who trust in him.

—ST. CATHERINE OF SIENA

5

Lose yourself wholly; and the more you lose,
the more you will find.

—ST. CATHERINE OF SIENA

6

All the way to heaven is heaven,
because Jesus said, "I am the way."

—ST. CATHERINE OF SIENA

7

_____

I do not understand how it is possible not to trust
in him who can do all things. With him, everything;
without him, nothing. He is Lord.

—ST. FAUSTINA KOWALSKA

8

MAY

Pray with great confidence, with confidence based on the goodness and infinite generosity of God and upon the promises of Jesus Christ.

—ST. LOUIS DE MONTFORT

9

I am the happiest of men for I serve the Lord through the poor and sick children rejected by everyone else.

—ST. DAMIEN OF MOLAKAI

10

There is great reason you should distrust yourself,
but there is much greater reason that you should
trust yourself entirely to your Divine Savior.

—ST. VINCENT DE PAUL

11

_____

_____

_____

_____

_____

_____

_____

Should we fall in a sin, let us humble ourselves
orrowfully in His presence, and then, with an act of
unbounded confidence, let us throw ourselves into
the ocean of His goodness, where every failing will
be cancelled and every anxiety turned into love.

—ST. PAUL OF THE CROSS

12

_____

_____

_____

_____

_____

_____

_____

MAY

The message of Fatima is, in its basic meaning, a call to conversion and repentance, as in the Gospel . . . The call to repentance is a motherly one, and at the same time, it is strong and decisive.

—ST. JOHN PAUL II

13

In sorrow and suffering, go straight to God with confidence, and you will be strengthened, enlightened, and instructed.

—ST. JOHN OF THE CROSS

14

Faith renders meaningless such words as anxiety, danger, and fear, so that the believer goes through life calmly and peacefully, with profound joy— like a child hand in hand with his mother.

—BLESSED CHARLES DE FOUCAULD

15

There is no more excellent way to obtain graces from God than to seek them through Mary, because her divine Son cannot refuse her anything.

—ST. PHILIP NERI

16

MAY

Rich is the mercy of our God, and abundantly does he bestow grace upon grace on those who love him.

—ST. ELIZABETH OF SCHÖNAU

17

[Our Lord] would not so urge and almost force us to pray to him if he had not a most eager desire to bestow his graces on us.

—ST. JOHN CHRYSOSTOM

18

Grace is the light by which men see the way to walk
out of sin; and grace is the staff without whose help
no man is able to rise out of sin.

—ST. THOMAS MORE

19

The Name of Jesus is the most sweet-tasting
nourishment of contemplation, for it feeds
and revives those souls that are famished
and spiritually hungry.

—ST. BERNARDINE OF SIENA

20

MAY

If Christ is with us, who is against us? You can fight with confidence where you are sure of victory. With Christ and for Christ victory is certain.

—ST. BERNARD OF CLAIRVAUX

21

No matter what efforts I make, I cannot die to myself without his grace. I am like a frog which, no matter how high it leaps, always finishes up in the mud. . . . Draw me then, O Lord, draw me after you.

—ST. DOMINIC BARBERI

22

Christ patiently awaits the return of the sinner, and he gently receives the penitent. This twofold mercy abounds in the heart of the Lord Jesus— his long-suffering in waiting for the sinner and his readiness in granting pardon.

—ST. BERNARD OF CLAIRVAUX

23

Rejoicing and eternal praise be to you, my Lord Jesus Christ, who sent the Holy Spirit into the hearts of your disciples.

—ST. BRIDGET OF SWEDEN

24

MAY

Let grace be the beginning,
grace the consummation, grace the crown.

—ST. BEDE

25

If you wish to go to extremes, let it be in sweetness,
patience, humility and charity.

—ST. PHILIP NERI

26

O the mercy of God! Never does he refuse
to be merciful, but is ever present to those
who turn to him.

—ST. ANTHONY OF PADUA

2 7

Mercy is a good thing, for it makes men perfect,
in that it imitates the perfect Father.
Nothing graces the Christian soul so much as mercy.

—ST. AMBROSE

2 8

MAY

The new man, reborn and restored to his God by grace, says first of all, "Father!" because he has now begun to be a son.

—ST. CYPRIAN

29

I believe that I shall be saved . . . even though my sins from the time of my childhood, and those I have committed up to this present hour, are very great, for your mercy is greater than the malice of my sins.

—ST. FRANCIS XAVIER

30

> You must be like [Mary], giving in haste the word you have received in meditation.
>
> —ST. TERESA OF CALCUTTA

31

PRAYER NOTES

MAY

JUNE

Nothing apart from God can satisfy the human heart that is truly in search of him.

—ST. ANTHONY OF PADUA

Impelled by the desire of the eternal and pure life,
we seek the abode that is with God,
the Father and Creator of all.

—ST. JUSTIN MARTYR

1

Live in such a way that all may know that you bear
outwardly as well as inwardly the image of Christ
crucified, the model of all gentleness and mercy.

—ST. PAUL OF THE CROSS

2

God, the Creator of all things, is so full of mercy
and compassion that whatever may be the grace
for which we stretch out our hands,
we shall not fail to receive it.

—ST. BERNARD OF CLAIRVAUX

3

In her voyage across the ocean of this world,
the Church is like a great ship being pounded by the
waves of life's different stresses. Our duty is not to
abandon ship but to keep her on her course.

—ST. BONIFACE

4

What we ourselves cannot bear let us bear with the help of Christ. For he is all-powerful and he tells us: My yoke is easy and my burden is light.

—ST. BONIFACE

5

The word of God is inflamed with the fire of the Holy Spirit. It consumes vices and promotes virtue. It bestows wisdom on well-disposed people and provides for them heavenly food.

—ST. NORBERT

6

Only by the means of grace can nature be liberated
from its dross, restored to its purity, and made
free to receive divine life.

—ST. TERESA BENEDICTA OF THE CROSS
(EDITH STEIN)

7

How precious the gift of the cross, how splendid to
contemplate! In the cross there is no mingling of
good and evil, as in the tree of paradise: it is wholly
beautiful to behold and good to taste. The fruit of
this tree is not death but life, not darkness, but light.

—ST. THEODORE THE STUDITE

8

JUNE

Virtues are formed by prayer. Prayer preserves temperance. Prayer suppresses anger. Prayer prevents emotions of pride and envy. Prayer draws into the soul the Holy Spirit, and raises man to Heaven.

—ST. EPHREM

9

As through a tree we were made debtors to God, so through a tree we receive the cancellation of our debt.

—ST. IRENAEUS

10

Prayer means a launching out of the heart towards God; it means lifting up one's eyes, quite simply, to heaven, a cry of grateful love, from the crest of joy or the trough of despair.

—ST. THÉRÈSE OF LISIEUX

11

I do not advise you to say many words in prayer . . . In prayer, hold yourself before God like a poor mute man and a paralytic at the door of a rich man, and spend your time keeping your soul in the presence of the Lord.

—BROTHER LAWRENCE

12

JUNE

The kingdom of God is the highest good:
the is why it is to be sought.

—ST. ANTHONY OF PADUA

13

_____

It is only in adversity that we come to know whether
we have made real progress in goodness.

—ST. ANTHONY OF PADUA

14

Nothing apart from God can satisfy the human heart
that is truly in search of him.

—ST. ANTHONY OF PADUA

15

_____

_____

_____

_____

_____

_____

_____

_____

Whatever our bodies may be doing, we should at
the same time continually lift up our minds to God,
which is the most acceptable form of prayer.

—ST. THOMAS MORE

16

_____

_____

_____

_____

_____

_____

_____

JUNE

Don't let a day go by without praying a little!
Prayer is a duty, but it is also a joy because it is
a dialogue with God through Jesus Christ.

—POPE ST. JOHN PAUL II

17

It gives more praise to God and more delight
if we pray steadfast in love, trusting his goodness,
clinging to him by grace, than if we ask for
everything our thoughts can name.

—BLESSED JULIAN OF NORWICH

18

Realize above all that you are in God's presence. . . .
Empty yourself completely and sit waiting,
content with the grace of God, like a chick who
tastes nothing and eats nothing but what
his mother brings him.

—ST. ROMUALD

19

Let your prayer be completely simple, for both the
publican and the prodigal son were reconciled to
God by a single phrase.

—ST. JOHN CLIMACUS

20

JUNE

It is better to be the child of God than king of the whole world.

—ST. ALOYSIUS GONZAGA

21

Give me, good Lord, such a love for you
that I will love nothing in a way that displeases you,
and I will love everything for your sake.

—ST. THOMAS MORE

22

The more you pray, the more you want to pray. . . . It's like a fish that starts by swimming near the surface of the water, then plunges. . . . The soul plunges, is swallowed up, and loses itself in the delights of conversation with God.

—ST. JOHN VIANNEY

23

He must increase; I must decrease.

—ST. JOHN THE BAPTIST (JOHN 3:30)

24

JUNE

You don't need to use many or high-sounding words. Just repeat often, "Lord, show me your mercy as you know best." Or, "God, come to my assistance."

—ST. MACARIUS OF ALEXANDRIA

2 5

Aspire to God with short but frequent outpourings of the heart; admire his bounty; invoke his aid; cast yourself in spirit at the foot of the cross; adore his goodness; treat with him of your salvation; give him your whole soul a thousand times in the day.

—ST. FRANCIS DE SALES

2 6

The body of Christ gives life to those who partake of it. For it expels death, whenever it comes to be in those who are dying, and expels corruption.

—ST. CYRIL OF ALEXANDRIA

27

God did not tell us to follow him because he needed our help, but because he knew that loving him would make us whole.

—ST. IRENAEUS

28

JUNE

Every moment of prayer, especially before our Lord in the tabernacle, is a sure, positive gain. The time we spend in having our daily audience with God is the most precious part of the whole day.

—ST. TERESA OF CALCUTTA

29

Prayer is the most powerful weapon a Christian has. Prayer makes us effective. Prayer makes us happy. Prayer gives us all the strength we need to fulfill God's commands. Yes, indeed, your whole life can and should be prayer.

—ST. JOSEMARÍA ESCRIVÁ

30

PRAYER NOTES

JUNE

JULY

All my life, I have . . . wanted to carry the gospel message to those who have never heard of God.

—ST. JUNÍPERO SERRA

All my life, I have . . . wanted to carry the gospel message to those who have never heard of God.

—ST. JUNÍPERO SERRA

1

Sometimes, during my hours of prayer, I picture mysel as a piece of stone before a sculptor who intends to make a statue out of it. Presenting myself like this before the Lord, I beg him to form in my soul his perfect image and make me wholly like Christ.

—BROTHER LAWRENCE

2

Sometimes when I find myself spiritually in dryness so great that I cannot produce a single good thought, I recite very slowly an Our Father or a Hail Mary. These prayers alone console me. . . . They nourish my soul.

—ST. THÉRÈSE OF LISIEUX

3

God made me queen so that I may serve others.

—ST. ELIZABETH OF PORTUGAL

4

JULY

We should love and feel compassion for those who oppose us, . . . since they harm themselves and do us good, and adorn us with crowns of everlasting glory

—ST. ANTHONY MARIA ZACCARIA

5

We would all much better mend our ways if we were as ready to pray for one another as we are to offer one another reproach and rebuke.

—ST. THOMAS MORE

6

It can only be disgraceful for some Christians to
snore while other Christians are in peril.

—ST. THOMAS MORE

7

Give me a sense of humor, Lord,
and something to laugh about.

—ST. THOMAS MORE

8

JULY

Occupy your mind with good thoughts,
or the enemy will fill them with bad ones.
Unoccupied they cannot be.

—ST. THOMAS MORE

9

I will remember how Saint Peter . . . began to sink
because of his lack of faith, and I will do as he did:
call upon Christ.

—ST. THOMAS MORE

10

Never give a hollow greeting of peace or turn away
when someone needs your love.

—ST. BENEDICT

11

The present is nothing. But eternity abides
for those on whom all truth, all good,
has shone in one entire and perfect light.

—ST. PAULINUS OF NOLA

12

JULY

> Present glory is fleeting and meaningless
> while it is possessed, unless in it
> we can glimpse something of heaven's eternity.
>
> —ST. HENRY

13

_____
_____
_____
_____
_____
_____
_____
_____

> Follow Christ; do good and avoid evil;
> live the life of heaven on earth.
>
> —ST. PAULINUS OF NOLA

14

_____
_____
_____
_____
_____
_____
_____
_____

God created all things not to increase his glory,
but to show it forth and to communicate it.

—ST. BONAVENTURE

15

Of what use are riches in eternity?

—ST. ALOYSIUS GONZAGA

16

JULY

We must love prayer. It widens the heart to the point of making it capable of containing the gift that God makes of himself.

—ST. TERESA OF CALCUTTA

17

_____
_____
_____
_____

_____
_____
_____
_____
_____

Think well. Speak well. Do well.
These three things, through the mercy of God,
will make a man go to heaven.

—ST. CAMILLUS DE LELLIS

18

_____
_____
_____

_____
_____
_____
_____
_____

Cast away your troublesome cares; put aside your wearisome distractions. Give yourself a little leisure to talk to God, and rest awhile in him.

—ST. ANSELM

19

Prayer is a treasure undiminished, a mine never exhausted, a sky unobstructed by clouds, a haven unruffled by storm. . . . Prayer is the anchor of those tossed on the sea, the treasure of the poor, the cure of diseases, the safeguard of health.

—ST. JOHN CHRYSOSTOM

20

JULY

All things are possible for him who believes, more to him who hopes, even more to him who loves.

—ST. LAWRENCE OF BRINDISI

21

If you avoid unnecessary talk and aimless visits, listening to news and gossip, you will find plenty of suitable time to spend in meditation on holy things.

—THOMAS À KEMPIS

22

The world would have peace if only men of politics
would follow the Gospels.

—ST. BRIDGET OF SWEDEN

23

Blessed be he who by his love has given life to all.
To him be the glory.

—ST. SHARBEL MAKHLUF'S LAST PRAYER

24

JULY

Anyone who has not begun to pray, I beg,
for love of the Lord, not to miss so great a blessing.
There is no place here for fear, but only desire.

—ST. TERESA OF ÁVILA

25

Communion is the life of your soul. If you were to
eat only one meal each week, would you survive?
It's the same thing with your soul: you must nourish
your soul with the Holy Eucharist.

—ST. ANDRÉ BESSETTE

26

Expect much of God, and he will do much for you.

—ST. BERNARD OF CLAIRVAUX

_____

_____ **27**

_____

_____

_____

_____

_____

Give me only your love and your grace, and
I am rich enough and ask for nothing more.

—ST. IGNATIUS OF LOYOLA

_____

_____ **28**

_____

_____

_____

_____

_____ **JULY**

He who wants to overcome vices should fight
with the arms of love, not of rage.

—ST. PETER CHRYSOLOGUS

29

Peace is the plenitude that fulfills our desires.
As Christ left the world, he wished to leave the gift
he wanted to find when he returned.

—ST. PETER CHRYSOLOGUS

30

> As long as obedience is flourishing, all the other virtues will be seen to flourish and to bear fruit.
>
> —ST. IGNATIUS OF LOYOLA

31

PRAYER NOTES

JULY

AUGUST

God commands you to pray,
but he forbids you to worry.

—ST. JOHN VIANNEY

> Nothing can satisfy one whom God does not satisfy.
>
> —ST. ALPHONSUS LIGUORI

1

_____

_____

_____

_____

_____

_____

_____

_____

> Is [Our Lord] not always the Good Shepherd, the Divine Consoler, the Changeless Friend?
>
> —ST. PETER JULIAN EYMARD

2

_____

_____

_____

_____

_____

_____

_____

We must desire our neighbor's good and rejoice
when he obtains it. And on the other hand,
we must be sorry for his misfortunes.

—ST. ALPHONSUS LIGUORI

3

_____

_____

_____

_____

_____

_____

_____

_____

Nothing is so beautiful as a pure soul. . . .
Purify yourselves then by a good confession.

—ST. JOHN VIANNEY

4

_____

_____

_____

_____

_____

_____

_____

AUGUST

God commands you to pray,
but he forbids you to worry.

—ST. JOHN VIANNEY

5

The Transfiguration shows us clearly not only Jesus'
glory but the glory to which we ourselves are called.

—FR. FRANCIS MARTIN

6

We can, if we will, become a saint,
for God will never refuse to help us to do so.

—ST. JOHN VIANNEY

7

A man who governs his passions is master
of the world. We must either command them,
or be enslaved to them.

—ST. DOMINIC

8

AUGUST

Whenever you seek truth, you seek God,
whether or not you know it.

**—ST. TERESA BENEDICTA OF THE CROSS
(EDITH STEIN)**

9

It is not human activity that can help us,
but the Passion of Christ.

**—ST. TERESA BENEDICTA OF THE CROSS
(EDITH STEIN)**

10

Love God, serve God; everything is in that.

—ST. CLARE OF ASSISI

_____
_____
_____ **11**
_____
_____
_____
_____
_____
_____

Whatever good or evil befalls you, be confident
that God will convert it all to your good.

—ST. JANE FRANCES DE CHANTAL

_____
_____
_____ **12**
_____
_____
_____
_____
_____

AUGUST

Christ, like a skillful physician, understands the weakness of men. He loves to teach the ignorant and the erring he turns again to his own true way.

—ST. HIPPOLYTUS

13

The most resplendent manifestation of God's glory is the salvation of souls, whom Christ redeemed by shedding his blood.

—ST. MAXIMILIAN MARY KOLBE

14

O blessed day that saw the humble handmaid of the Lord raised and borne aloft to such great glory, . . . by the side of Christ, enthroned in the kingdom of the blessed!

—ST. PETER CANASIUS

15

Do not show favor only to relations and kin, or to the most eminent . . . Show favor to all who come to you. By fulfilling your duty in this way, you will reach the highest state of happiness.

—ST. STEPHEN OF HUNGARY

16

AUGUST

If you are told, as was the Canaanite woman, that you do not deserve the grace for which you are asking, then reply like her that you are not seeking unusual favors, but are hoping only to eat the crumbs which fall from the divine table.

—ST. JANE FRANCES DE CHANTAL

17

Jesus is my All, and I desire to belong wholly to him. It is extreme folly and delusion to look elsewhere for any true happiness.

—ST. JOHN EUDES

18

When [God] gives you grace, you must not think
that he gives it to you in answer to your prayers,
but rather that he gives it to his Son Jesus Christ
by virtue of his prayers and merits.

—ST. JOHN EUDES

19

_____

That man is truly humble who converts
humiliation into humility.

—ST. BERNARD OF CLAIRVAUX

20

AUGUST

Every day we ask God for the bread to sustain
the life of our body. So, too, we have need
of heavenly Bread that gives life to our soul.

—ST. PIUS X

21

_____

The Blessed Virgin Mary should be called Queen . . .
because God has willed her to have an exceptional
role in the work of our eternal salvation.

—POPE PIUS XII

22

_____

The gift of grace increases as the struggle increases.

—ST. ROSE OF LIMA

_____

_____ **23**

_____

_____

_____

_____

_____

_____

I need nothing but God and to lose myself
in the heart of Jesus.

—ST. MARGARET MARY ALACOQUE

_____

_____ **24**

_____

_____

_____

_____

_____

_____

AUGUST

In prosperity, give thanks to God with humility
and fear lest by pride you abuse
God's benefits and so offend him.

—ST. LOUIS OF FRANCE

25

God does all he can, without taking away
our free will . . . to change suffering from
something that crushes and destroys us into
something that exalts and renews us.

—CARYLL HOUSELANDER

26

Son, . . . I do not know what there is now for me to do or why I am still here, all my hopes in this world being now fulfilled.

—ST. MONICA, ABOUT THE CONVERSION OF ST. AUGUSTINE OF HIPPO

27

Let us understand that God is a physician, and that suffering is a medicine for salvation, not a punishment for damnation.

—ST. AUGUSTINE OF HIPPO

28

AUGUST

Look today to John the Baptist, an enduring model
of fidelity to God and his Law. . . . Imitate
him with docile and trusting generosity.

—POPE ST. JOHN PAUL II

29

Faith opens the door to understanding;
unbelief closes it.

—ST. AUGUSTINE OF HIPPO

30

The source of man's love for God can only be found
in the fact that God loved him first.

—ST. AUGUSTINE OF HIPPO

31

_____

_____

_____

_____

_____

_____

_____

PRAYER NOTES

_____

_____

_____

_____

_____

_____

_____

_____

_____

AUGUST

SEPTEMBER

God is more anxious to
bestow his blessings on us
than we are to receive them.

—ST. AUGUSTINE OF HIPPO

God is more anxious to bestow his blessings
on us than we are to receive them.

—ST. AUGUSTINE OF HIPPO

1

It remains for us all, each in his own measure,
to make known to those around us the mystery
of our new life in Christ.

—ST. GREGORY THE GREAT

2

> He causes his prayers to be of more avail to himself who offers them also for others.
>
> —ST. GREGORY THE GREAT

3

_____

> Christ does not force our will; he only takes what we give him. But he does not give himself entirely until he sees that we yield ourselves entirely to him.
>
> —ST. TERESA OF ÁVILA

4

SEPTEMBER

Few souls understand what God would accomplish in them if they were to abandon themselves unreservedly to him and if they were to allow his grace to mold them accordingly.

—ST. IGNATIUS OF LOYOLA

5

_____
_____
_____
_____
_____
_____
_____
_____
_____

God did not give us our free will to sin with, but to love with.

—CARYLL HOUSELANDER

6

_____
_____
_____
_____
_____
_____
_____
_____

Engrave on your hearts the words of the Lord that you hear. For the word of God is the food of the soul and should remain in our memory.

—ST. GREGORY THE GREAT

7

_____

Let us ask the Blessed Virgin Mary to open our hearts to greater confidence in the Lord who in her, the humble and docile handmaid, worked great wonders.

—ST. JOHN PAUL II

8

SEPTEMBER

Since gold and silver, which are only corruptible metals, are purified and tested by fire, it is but reasonable that our faith, which surpasses all the riches of the world, should be tried.

—ST. PETER CLAVER

9

Ah, Jesus, very closest to my heart, always be with me in such a way that my heart may abide with you and your love may indivisibly persevere with me.

—ST. GERTRUDE THE GREAT

10

Do not pursue spectacular deeds. . . . What matters is the gift of your self, the degree of love that you put into each one of your actions.

—ST. TERESA OF CALCUTTA

11

_____
_____
_____
_____
_____
_____
_____
_____

O name of Mary! Joy in the heart, honey in the mouth, melody in the ear of those devoted to her!

—ST. ANTHONY OF PADUA

12

_____
_____
_____
_____
_____
_____
_____

SEPTEMBER

Prayer has power to destroy whatever
is at enmity with the good.

—ST. JOHN CHRYSOSTOM

13

Glory be to you, who laid your Cross as a bridge
over death, that souls might pass over it from the
dwelling of the dead to the dwelling of life!

—ST. EPHREM

14

Silence, prayer, suffering, waiting: these are the lessons Our Lady is always teaching me.

—ST. MARY EUPHRASIA PELLETIER

15

_____
_____
_____
_____
_____
_____
_____
_____

To him who still remains in this world, no repentance is too late. The approach to God's mercy is open.

—ST. CYPRIAN

16

_____
_____
_____
_____
_____
_____

SEPTEMBER

It is . . . necessary for us to get into the way
of always and instinctively turning to God.

—ST. ROBERT BELLARMINE

17
_____
_____
_____
_____
_____
_____
_____
_____
_____

Charity is that with which no one is lost,
and without which no one is saved.

—ST. ROBERT BELLARMINE

18
_____
_____
_____
_____
_____
_____
_____

I beg you not to fail in your love for one another,
but to support one another and to stand fast until
the Lord mercifully delivers us from our trials.

—ST. ANDREW KIM TAEGON

19

The Lord is like a farmer and we are the field
of rice that he fertilizes with his grace
and by the mystery of the incarnation and the
redemption irrigates with his blood,
in order that we will grow and reach maturity.

—ST. ANDREW KIM TAEGON

20

SEPTEMBER

When I am incapable of praying, . . . I at least tell
[Jesus] again and again that I love Him; that is not
difficult, and it keeps alive the fire in my heart.

—ST. THÉRÈSE OF LISIEUX

21

The humble soul is like a grain of wheat thrown
into the earth: it descends, it hides itself,
it disappears, it dies; but to revive in heaven.

—ST. MARIAM BAOUARDY

22

Remember: The sinner who is sorry for his sins is closer to God than the just man who boasts of his good works.

—ST. PIO OF PIETRELCINA

23

The more you abandon to God the care of all temporal things, the more He will take care to provide for all your wants.

—ST. JOHN BAPTIST DE LA SALLE

24

SEPTEMBER

You must ask God to give you power to fight against the sin of pride which is your greatest enemy— the root of all that is evil, and the failure of all that is good. For God resists the proud.

—ST. VINCENT DE PAUL

25

The affairs of God are accomplished little by little and almost imperceptibly. The Spirit of God is neither violent nor hasty.

—ST. VINCENT DE PAUL

26

A good work talked about is a good work spoilt.

—ST. VINCENT DE PAUL

_____
_____
_____ **27**
_____
_____
_____
_____
_____

The angels, wherever they may be sent, never stop
gazing upon God. In the same way, the virtuous
person, as much as he can, always keeps
the memory of God in his heart.

—ST. BONAVENTURE

_____
_____
_____ **28**
_____
_____
_____
_____
_____

SEPTEMBER

An angel is put in charge of every believer,
provided we do not drive him out by sin.
He guards the soul like an army.

—ST. BASIL THE GREAT

29

It is not enough for me that God has given me grace
once, but He must give it always. I ask, that I may
receive; and when I have received, I ask again.

—ST. JEROME

30

PRAYER NOTES

SEPTEMBER

OCTOBER

I have been all things unholy. If God can work through me, he can work through anyone.

—ST. FRANCIS OF ASSISI

Your soul is in the arms of your divine spouse, like a baby in its mother's arms. You may sleep in peace, therefore, for this heavenly spouse will guide you in the way which is to your greatest advantage.

—ST. PIO OF PIETRELCINA

1

_____
_____
_____
_____
_____
_____
_____
_____

If you find it impossible to pray, hide behind your good Angel and charge him to pray in your stead.

—ST. JOHN VIANNEY

2

_____
_____
_____
_____
_____
_____
_____

I have been all things unholy. If God can work
through me, he can work through anyone.

—ST. FRANCIS OF ASSISI

_____

_____

_____   **3**

_____

_____

_____

_____

_____

It is no use walking anywhere to preach
unless our walking is our preaching.

—ST. FRANCIS OF ASSISI

_____

_____

_____   **4**

_____

_____

_____

_____

_____ **OCTOBER**

Oh, how happy is the soul that freely lets herself be molded to the liking of this divine Savior!

—ST. JANE FRANCES DE CHANTAL

5

Love God above all, so that warmed by his embrace you may be aflame with divine love.

—ST. BRUNO

6

The holy Rosary is a powerful weapon.
Use it with confidence and you will be
amazed at the results.

—ST. JOSEMARÍA ESCRIVÁ

7

During painful times, when you feel a terrible void,
think how God is enlarging the capacity of your soul
so that it can receive him—making it, as it were,
infinite, as he is infinite.

—ST. ELIZABETH OF THE TRINITY

8

OCTOBER

Eternal God, . . . I offer you all my thoughts, words, and actions of this day . . . for love of you, for your glory, to fulfill your divine will.

—ST. JOHN LEONARDI

9

Be diligent in serving the poor.
Love the poor, honor them,
as you would honor Christ himself.

—ST. LOUISE DE MARILLAC

10

The surrendered soul has found paradise on earth, since she enjoys that sweet peace which is part of the happiness of the elect.

—ST. MARIE-VICTOIRE COUDERC

11

Holiness does not demand anything great, beyond the ability of the person. It depends on God's love; every daily act can be transformed into an act of love.

—ST. URSULA LEDÓCHOWSKA

12

OCTOBER

In speaking of others be always calm and cheerful.

—ST. TERESA OF ÁVILA

13

_____

_____

_____

_____

_____

_____

_____

_____

Let nothing disturb you, nothing frighten you;
all things are passing; God only is changeless.

—ST. TERESA OF ÁVILA

14

_____

_____

_____

_____

_____

_____

_____

You pay God a compliment by
asking great things of him.

—ST. TERESA OF ÁVILA

15

_____

O Jesus, my most sincere friend: come to my aid
according to the magnitude of your mercies.

—ST. MARGARET MARY ALACOQUE

16

OCTOBER

Be eager for more frequent gatherings for thanksgivin
to God and for his glory. For when you meet frequent
the forces of Satan are annulled and his destructive
power is canceled in the concord of your faith.

—ST. IGNATIUS OF ANTIOCH

17

A Christian is not his own master,
since all his time belongs to God.

—ST. IGNATIUS OF ANTIOCH

18

Our single endeavor should be to give ourselves
to the work and to be faithful to him,
and not to spoil his work by our shortcomings.

—ST. ISAAC JOGUES

19

Let us throw ourselves into the ocean
of his goodness, where every failing
will be canceled and anxiety turned into love.

—ST. PAUL OF THE CROSS

20

OCTOBER

The Cross is the way to Paradise,
but only when it is borne willingly.

—ST. PAUL OF THE CROSS

21

When you feel the assaults of passion and anger,
then is the time to be silent as Jesus was silent in
the midst of His ignominies and sufferings.

—ST. PAUL OF THE CROSS

22

Priests have been placed here to care of others.
Their own lives should be an example to others,
showing how they must live in the house
of the Lord.

—ST. JOHN OF CAPISTRANO

23

My God, give me a zeal that is discreet and prudent
so that I may do everything strongly yet sweetly,
gently yet thoroughly.

—ST. ANTHONY MARY CLARET

24

OCTOBER

At night when you retire to rest, take your beads and go off to sleep while saying them; do the same as little children who fall asleep saying, "Mamma, Mamma."

—ST. BERNADETTE SOUBIROUS

25

Apart from the cross there is no other ladder by which we may get to heaven.

—ST. ROSE OF LIMA

26

What an extraordinary thing it is, the efficiency of prayer! Like a queen, it has access at all times to the royal Presence, and can get whatever it asks for.

—ST. THÉRÈSE OF LISIEUX

27

_____

_____

_____

_____

_____

_____

A little drop of simple obedience is worth a million times more than a whole vase of the choicest contemplation.

—ST. MARY MAGDALENE DE PAZZI

28

_____

_____

_____

_____

_____

_____

OCTOBER

As in heaven your will is punctually performed,
so may it be done on earth by all creatures,
particularly in me and by me.

—ST. ELIZABETH OF HUNGARY

29

When a person loves another dearly, he desires
strongly to be close to the other: therefore,
why be afraid to die? Death brings us to God!

—ST. JOSEPHINE BAKHITA

30

In order to bring true peace back to my soul,
the only way that there exists on the Earth is
Confession, because Jesus awaits me
with His immense heart.

—ST. GIANNA BERETTA MOLLA

31

_____
_____
_____
_____
_____
_____
_____
_____

PRAYER NOTES

_____
_____
_____
_____
_____
_____
_____
_____
_____
_____
_____
_____
_____

NOVEMBER

Whoever surrenders unconditionally to the Lord will be chosen by him as an instrument for building his kingdom.

—ST. TERESA BENEDICTA OF THE CROSS (EDITH STEIN)

Make up your mind to become a saint.

—ST. MARY MAZZARELLO

1

_____

_____

_____

_____

_____

_____

_____

_____

We have to serve God in His way, not in ours.

—ST. TERESA OF ÁVILA

2

_____

_____

_____

_____

_____

_____

_____

_____

However severe God's guidance may seem to us at times, it's always the guidance of a Father who is infinitely good, wise, and kind. He leads us to our goal by different paths.

—ST. JULIA BILLIART

3

Be sure you first preach by the way you live.

—ST. CHARLES BORROMEO

4

NOVEMBER

God wishes us not to rest upon anything
but His infinite goodness.

—ST. CHARLES BORROMEO

5

_____

_____

_____

_____

_____

_____

_____

_____

May my soul never cease to praise the Lord
who never ceases to lavish gifts.

—ST. CHARLES BORROMEO

6

_____

_____

_____

_____

_____

_____

_____

_____

There are moments in life of special importance, such as when the Lord shows us the way to be followed and then leaves it up to our will to respond.

—BLESSED MARGARITA DE MATURANA

7

_____
_____
_____
_____
_____
_____
_____
_____

Know that gratitude for God's benefits is one of the riches of the soul and that ingratitude dries up the fountain of divine graces. Give your tribute of gratitude often to the most loving Jesus.

—ST. FRANCES XAVIER CABRINI

8

_____
_____
_____
_____
_____
_____
_____

NOVEMBER

No one should be ashamed of the cross of Christ,
through which the world has been redeemed.

—ST. LEO THE GREAT

9

_____

_____

_____

_____

_____

_____

_____

_____

_____

God wanted to set us free, and the way he
chose was to become one of us.

—ST. LEO THE GREAT

10

_____

_____

_____

_____

_____

_____

_____

Blessed is the soul who trusts in Jesus
because he is lavish in his promises and
generous in giving his graces and treasures.

—ST. FRANCES XAVIER CABRINI

11

Convert me, Jesus, convert me completely to
yourself, for if you do not make me a saint, I will
not know how to work in your vineyard.

—ST. FRANCES XAVIER CABRINI

12

NOVEMBER

Give me a heart as big as the universe!

—ST. FRANCES XAVIER CABRINI

13

_____
_____
_____
_____
_____
_____
_____
_____
_____

What a gift prayer is! It is the real treasure
of our soul, our being able to give to God
the worship of perfect adoration.

—ST. FRANCES XAVIER CABRINI

14

_____
_____
_____
_____
_____
_____
_____
_____

The greater and more persistent your confidence in God, the more abundantly you will receive all that you ask.

—ST. ALBERT THE GREAT

15

_____

O most loving Jesus, protect me beneath the shadow of your hand; let your right hand sustain me.

—ST. GERTRUDE THE GREAT

16

NOVEMBER

[The Israelites] were severely forbidden to gather more manna than they needed for one day. Do not doubt that God will provide for the next day, and all the days of our pilgrimage.

—ST. PIO OF PIETRELCINA

17

The trials ahead will never be as great as the help I may confidently expect from him.

—ST. ROSE PHILIPPINE DUCHESNE

18

We cultivate a very small field for Christ,
but we love it, knowing that God does not
require great achievements but a heart
that holds back nothing for self.

—ST. ROSE PHILIPPINE DUCHESNE

19

Humility is the virtue that requires
the greatest amount of effort.

—ST. ROSE PHILIPPINE DUCHESNE

20

NOVEMBER

Mary appears to us today as the temple in which God has placed his salvation and as the handmaid who was totally consecrated to the Lord.

—ST. JOHN PAUL II

21

To die for Christ is not to sacrifice one's youth, but to renew it. Jesus Christ returns a hundredfold for all offered him, and adds to it eternal life.

—ST. CECILIA

22

He who fashioned us and created us brought us into his world. Since, then, we owe all this to him, we ought to give him thanks for everything.

—ST. CLEMENT I

23

_____

_____

_____

_____

_____

_____

_____

_____

The blood of martyrs is for you, Christians in Vietnam, a wellspring of grace to make progress in the faith. In you, the faith of our fathers continues and is carried on to new generations.

—ST. JOHN PAUL II

24

_____

_____

_____

_____

_____

_____

NOVEMBER

Exercise pleasantness toward all, taking great care
that what you have commanded may
never be done by reason of force.

—ST. ANGELA MERICI

25

I am nourished by your will, O Mighty One!
Your will is the goal of my existence.

—ST. FAUSTINA KOWALSKA

26

Whoever surrenders unconditionally to the Lord
will be chosen by him as an instrument
for building his kingdom.

—ST. TERESA BENEDICTA OF THE CROSS
(EDITH STEIN)

27

More than anything else
I believe in the power of prayer.

—VENERABLE EDEL QUINN

28

NOVEMBER

You must never ask Jesus to wait.

—ST. URSULA LEDÓCHOWSKA

29

After Andrew spends the entire day with Jesus, he does not keep the treasure for his personal benefit, but hastens to share it with his brothers.

—ST. JOHN CHRYSOSTOM

30

PRAYER NOTES

_____

_____

_____

_____

_____

_____

_____

_____

_____

_____

_____

_____

_____

_____

_____

_____

_____

_____

_____

_____

_____

_____

_____

_____

_____

NOVEMBER

DECEMBER

God's Son became human
so that human beings might
have their home in God.

—ST. HILDEGARD OF BINGEN

Prayer is an uplifting of the heart . . .
a cry of gratitude and love.

—ST. THÉRÈSE OF LISIEUX

1

You must refuse nothing you recognize
to be his will.

—ST. JANE FRANCES DE CHANTAL

2

I love you, not because you have the power to give heaven or hell, but simply because you are you— my king and my God.

—ST. FRANCIS XAVIER

3

Every action of Christ and all his working of miracles were truly very great and divine and wonderful, but of all things the most wonderful is his honorable cross.

—ST. JOHN OF DAMASCUS

4

DECEMBER

Every year Advent reminds us that grace,
and that is God's will to save man,
is more powerful than sin.

—ST. JOHN PAUL II

5

Lord, do not let my heart lean either to the right or
to the left, but let your good Spirit guide me along
the straight path.

—ST. JOHN OF DAMASCUS

6

To the good man, to die is gain. The foolish fear death as the greatest of evils; the wise desire it as a rest after labors and the end of ills.

—ST. AMBROSE

7

The knowledge that God gives us of the Immaculate Conception of the Blessed Virgin should cause us to glorify him eternally for this masterpiece of his omnipotence in a nature that is purely human.

—ST. LOUISE DE MARILLAC

8

DECEMBER

Do not be frightened or grieve, or let your heart be dismayed. Am I not here? I, who am your Mother? And is not my help a refuge?

—OUR LADY TO ST. JUAN DIEGO

9

_____

_____

_____

_____

_____

_____

_____

_____

Jesus, the incarnate Wisdom! Beautiful from all eternity, he is the splendor of his Father, the unspotted mirror and image of his goodness.

—ST. LOUIS DE MONTFORT

10

_____

_____

_____

_____

_____

_____

_____

He who makes rich is made poor;
he takes on the poverty of my flesh,
that I may gain the riches of his divinity.

—ST. GREGORY NAZIANZEN

11

I am a compassionate mother to you and to all
of my devoted children who will call upon me
with confidence.

—OUR LADY TO ST. JUAN DIEGO

12

DECEMBER

Those whose hearts are pure
are temples of the Holy Spirit.

—ST. LUCY

13

God is more pleased by one work, however small,
done secretly, without desire that it be known, tha
a thousand done with desire that men know of the

—ST. JOHN OF THE CROSS

14

The soul that journeys to God, but doesn't shake off ts cares and quiet its appetites, is like someone who drags a cart uphill.

—ST. JOHN OF THE CROSS

15

Advent is "the springtime of love," when the soul awaits her Lover, knowing deep down that he is coming and that he will make her his own!

—CATHERINE DE HUECK DOHERTY

16

DECEMBER

Advent is such a beautiful season.
It is a time for renewal; it is especially
a time for forgiveness because God brings his
forgiveness to us in the shape of his Son.

—CATHERINE DE HUECK DOHERTY

17

Charity to the afflicted must be dear to the heart of
Jesus, who knew so well how to sorrow with those
he loved. I hope we shall ever bear this in mind.

—ST. MARY MACKILLOP

18

The Son of God became man so that the sons of men,
he sons of Adam, might become sons of God. . . . He
is the Son of God by nature; we, by grace.

—ST. ATHANASIUS

_____

_____

_____ **19**

_____

_____

_____

_____

_____

_____

In a word, to surrender oneself is to die to
everything and to self, to be no longer concerned
with self except to keep it continually
turned toward God.

—ST. MARIE-VICTOIRE COUDERC

_____

_____

_____ **20**

_____

_____

_____

_____

_____ **DECEMBER**

O Jesus, I promise you to submit myself
to all that you permit to happen to me;
make me only know your will.

—ST. GIANNA BERETTA MOLLA

21

The lesser he became through his human nature,
the greater was his goodness; the more he lowered
himself for me, the dearer he is to me.

—ST. BERNARD OF CLAIRVAUX

22

ight all error, but do it with good humor, patience, indness, and love. Harshness will damage your own soul and spoil the best cause.

—ST. JOHN OF KANTY

2 3

Ve desire to be able to welcome Jesus at Christmas time, not in a cold manger of our heart, but in a eart full of love and humility, in a heart so pure, so immaculate, so warm with love for one another.

—ST. TERESA OF CALCUTTA

2 4

DECEMBER

Look at him: He who holds the universe in his fist
is held in a narrow manger.

—ST. JEROME

25

Christmas also reveals the full meaning of every
human birth, and the joy which accompanies the Birth
of the Messiah is thus seen to be the foundation and
fulfillment of joy at every child born into the world.

—ST. JOHN PAUL II

26

God's Son became human, in order that human
beings might have their home in God.

—ST. HILDEGARD OF BINGEN

27

Let us ask the Holy Innocents to help us . . .
to offer up our own pain and to have great
compassion for all who suffer.

—FRANCIS FERNANDEZ

28

DECEMBER

Into your hands, O Lord, I commend my spirit! . . .
For the name of Jesus and in defense of the Church
I am willing to die.

—ST. THOMAS BECKET

29

The object of a New Year is not that we should have
a new year. It is that we should have a new soul.

—G. K. CHESTERTON

30

Only a few hours more, and this year too will come
to an end . . . I go down on my knees before my God
and, recalling his kindnesses to me this year, I humble
myself in the dust and thank him with all my heart.

—ST. JOHN XXIII

31

PRAYER NOTES

DECEMBER

PRAYER NOTES

PRAYER NOTES

_____
_____
_____
_____
_____
_____
_____
_____
_____
_____
_____
_____
_____
_____
_____
_____
_____
_____
_____
_____
_____
_____
_____
_____
_____
_____
_____

the WORD among us®

The *Spirit* of Catholic Living

This book was published by The Word Among Us. Since 19
The Word Among Us has been answering the call of the Secon
Vatican Council to help Catholic laypeople encounter Christ
the Scriptures.

The name of our company comes from the prologue to the Gosp
John and reflects the vision and purpose of all of our publications:
an instrument of the Spirit, whose desire is to manifest Jesus' pres
in and to the children of God. In this way, we hope to contribu
the Church's ongoing mission of proclaiming the gospel to the w
so that all people would know the love and mercy of our Lord
grow more deeply in their faith as missionary disciples.

Our monthly devotional magazine, *The Word Among Us*, fea
meditations on the daily and Sunday Mass readings and curr
reaches more than one million Catholics in North America and an
half-million Catholics in one hundred countries around the world.
book division, The Word Among Us Press, publishes numerous b
Bible studies, and pamphlets that help Catholics grow in their fa

To learn more about who we are and what we publish, visit
www.wau.org. There you will find a variety of Catholic resources
will help you grow in your faith.

Embrace His Word, Listen to God . .